Badge

Or

Beast

*Written by
Bennie Watson*

Copyright © 2017

Bennie Watson

Revised May 2018

Bethune Publishing House

The Bethune Group MMB, Inc

All rights reserved, including the right to reproduce this work in any form whatsoever without written permission from the publisher, except for brief passages in connection with a review. Photographs may not be reproduced without permission of the owner.

For information write:

Bethune Publishing House, Inc.

P. O. Box 2008

Daytona Beach, FL 32115-2008

docbethune@tbginc.org

Jacket designed by John-Mark McLeod

J2maginations, LLC

J2maginations@gmail.com

Book design and page layout by

Bethune Publishing House, Inc.

Printed in the United States of America

Library of Congress Control Number: 2017909406
ISBN: 9781946566027

About the Author

Bennie Watson started his Law Enforcement/ Corrections career in 1981. He worked in the Criminal Justice field for more than thirty years. Three as a Police Officer and twenty-seven as a Correctional Officer/Supervisor.

Mr. Watson worked as a Police Officer with the Orlando Police Department, the Eatonville Police Department, Winter Park Police Department (Florida), Orange County Sheriff's Department (Orlando, Fla.) and The Orange County Corrections Department (Orlando, FL). He retired a Corrections Sergeant from Orange County Corrections on January 31, 2010.

Having earned a Master's Degree in Strategic Leadership from Mountain State University (West Virginia) as well as a B.A. Degree in General Studies with a minor in Criminal Justice Administration, from Columbia College (Missouri), Mr. Watson is not just trained in the field of Law Enforcement but educated in the areas of leadership, policy development and implementation.

When Mr. Watson received his A.A. degree from Columbia College, in Criminal Justice Administration, maintaining a 3.37 grade point average, it opened the door to a desire to achieve more. He continued to maintain a 3.4 or above GPA with his Bachelor's and Master's degrees. As a Dean's List honors student, he completed more than 58 hours of study at Valencia College (Orlando) in Criminal Justice.

Bennie Watson retired in September 2002 from the United States Army Reserves after serving twenty-two (22 years) as a Medical Specialist (Combat Medic 91-Bravo).

When asked why he decided to write a book on this particular topic, Mr. Watson stated "I like a book I can read on a two or four-hour flight or one I can read in a day or two. Cops like to "KISS", *keep it simple stupid,* so I decided to write about what I know and answer questions that are asked of me all the time. I hope you enjoy my book and learn to recognize the changes in you or your love one's personality and get counseling if needed".

Introduction

Let me begin by clearing up some inherent misconceptions before I get into the meat of my book. It is very important for people to understand that I am writing my book from the perspective of being a Black officer. I know it may seem, at times, that it is a one-sided view. Some may think that I come across as being prejudiced when I compare the facts that white officers gunning down black kids seems to be the norm while the statistics will support the fact that Black officers gunning down white kids is unheard-of.

I am stating facts that are seldom considered as there is very little literature or commentary that deals with these issues through the eyes of the Black officer. I am speaking of what I have seen throughout my career from the perspective of being a Black officer. I know of and speak about a white officer at OPD gunning down (shooting) and killing a twenty-five-year-old Black man. This officer shot the Black man in the back, while he was running away from the officer. During the time of the shooting, it was "justified" by the law. The law stipulated that if someone committed a felony and decided to flee, (run), from law-enforcement officer, the officer could legally shoot and kill them. Yes, the officer could shoot the perpetrator even if it was in the back without "fear for their life" being a part of the equation.

I briefly mention this incident in my book because it is as relevant today as it was then. I talk about these difficult issues, seriously speaking and straight from the heart. I was not raised to be prejudiced. My mother (God bless her soul), was very religious (Pentecostal) and taught all eight of her children straight out of the Bible, to love everybody, treat people right, and to treat people the way you want to be treated. The Golden Rule was the standard in our house. "Do unto others as you would have them do unto you". In addition, she also taught us to judge people by the content of their character and not by the color of their skin. These words of Rev. Martin Luther King, Jr., were as important in my formulative years as the scriptures of the Bible.

It is critical and very important to me that you know my personality and my character and know that this book is written to inform as well as open the door for a very necessary dialog. It is written from the heart. It is important that as you read, you keep an open mind and knowing that I am a true and genuine person who is definitely not prejudice will, I hope, allow for your consideration of the perspective that I present here.

Now…let's continue my book and get to the meat of the matter.

This is a must-read book for Police Officers, Correctional Officers, their wives, families, significant others and anyone in The Law Enforcement, Corrections or Criminal Justice field.

Questions:

1. Why did the Officers in the "Rodney King" incident continue to beat him as in the video tape?

2. Why do some "white" Police Officer's go into "Black" sections of town and gun down "Black Kids"? You very seldom, if at all, hear of a Black officer going into white neighborhoods gunning down little white kids.

3. Why is it that when Police Officers are training, the videos and other training material used show most cases with the suspect being black and the Officer is white?

4. Why, when Police Officers are trained at the firing range, they train to shoot at black silhouette targets?

5. Why is the divorce rate so high in families of law Enforcement/Corrections/Criminal Justice related fields?

6. What makes Law Enforcement/Corrections /Criminal Justice and related fields/jobs, so stressful?

7. Why is it that in some law Enforcement Corrections/ Criminal Justice and related fields, Officers turn from upholding the law to abusing the law?

Some of these questions and others will be answered in this book. This book was initially started a while back. I had to update it with information on today's actions from Law Enforcement Officer's, from around the country. We often hear of white Police officers gunning down blacks and you very seldom, if ever, hear of black Police Officers gunning down whites, especially children.

In some instances, especially here in Florida, even citizens are gunning down blacks and getting away with it. Have you ever heard of the "Stand Your Ground" law? Does the name Trayvon Martin ring a bell in your head? It's sad that for over thirty years in Florida, the "Fleeing Felon Law" was in effect. No matter the circumstance, if a Police Officer knew or thought someone was a felon or had committed a felony, they could shoot and kill them. This applied even if the person was running away from them. Yes, even in the back.

Do you remember the McDuffy case in Miami? After several years of white Police Officers and some black officers gunning down many, many blacks, the law was changed. The change however occurred only after hundreds of blacks were gunned down and killed by Police Officers who felt justified by that stupid law.

In Florida, right now 2018, we have a law, that I deem stupid, which is called the Stand Your Ground law. This is a law that allows Police Officers to gun down blacks (usually black men/boys and teens), but it also allows citizens to gun down blacks (remember George Zimmerman) and get away with it, if they "feel" threatened fear for their lives. Skittles and a bottle of Arizona tea is far from life threatening

Okay, let me get back to the meat of the matter the book "Badge or Beast". To answer some of the questions as to why some Law enforcement officers go from " Badge to Beast".

A Little History

Let's start this book by speaking on some of the training techniques used to become a COP. Much of the training is performed in the classroom. Some at the firing range. Much, much more in the field (F.T.O.). Once you have completed the necessary classroom training hours, required by the Criminal Justice Standards and Training Commission. You then are certified to carry a firearm.

Let's look at the many Law Enforcement agencies in the United States and the World. There is the F.B.I., Secret Service, C.I.A., Military Police, State Police, City Police County Deputies, Drug Agents and many, many more.

I have pondered some of these questions in my mind. I started my Law Enforcement career with the Orlando Police Department. I was chosen over four hundred applicants. I attended the J.C. Stone Memorial Academy, from February 1981 to May 1981. During my training with the Orlando Police Department, I noticed many of the training films were old. Many of them showed "Black" suspects with the arresting officer being "White". There were also more white, male officers than women of any color.

Also, some of the films showed more crime happening in the black section of town than in predominately white section. In watching those films, I wondered if this might be the reason why so many officers are apprehensive about coming into predominantly black sections of the community and sometimes to the point where they are just down right scared. People usually respond and react to situations the way they are trained. The way you train is the way you perform. Could it be, that psychologically on a state and local level, these training films and systems inadvertently program officers to do certain things, or act a certain way, or react in a certain way under stress.

I often wondered why some white police officers are afraid to go into black neighborhoods. This leads me to mention a true case where a young black man was shot and killed in West Orlando, by a white police officer. The young man was shot in the back with a shotgun while running away from the officer. The sad thing is that the young black man had done absolutely nothing wrong. The white police officer was allegedly responding to an assistance call, in a housing project. The officer allegedly exited his patrol car with a shotgun in his hand. As he responded to the scene, he shot and killed the young black man, in the back, who was running away from him.

When I was training, in the academy, I was taught not to exit my vehicle in a housing project with shotgun in hand. This was due to the scattering effect produced by the shotgun when fired. Also, there was the possibility you could hit innocent bystanders if you fired the weapon. However, the case was ruled justified. I have nothing against the training I received from the Academy. I do feel the Academy had an excellent training program. However, during the time I attended the Academy, I questioned, in my own mind, why some of the training films showed more "Black" suspects in the scenarios and portraying the negative roles than their "White" counter parts. Most of the negatives I encountered were not racial at all.

One I recall, is when I finished the Police Academy and continued my training in the field. I trained with a Black Police Officer who, in my opinion was a good COP, but a bad trainer. He, in my opinion, tried to mold me into the type of COP he was. Aggressive, hyper, etc. I didn't want to be like him. I thought he was ignorant.

Getting back to the true story. He was a Black Police Officer who had gunned down a young black man and bragged about it. During my training with him, I asked him why he had shot the guy in the back and killed him. He had frisked him. He was running from the officer and his life was not in danger. He replied, "No prisoner is going to escape from me." He often bragged about being a COP in New York and the military (Fort Brag). He felt he was tough and I was too passive. Again, I thought he was an A_ _ hole. When he told me why he shot and killed the young black man. I immediately lost all respect for him, as a trainer, and a human being.

To illustrate my point that not all incidents are racially motivated. I wonder if this officer sometimes thought he was white, at the time, he was married to a white woman. He told me, as a black officer, I had to put out 110%. I asked him why he felt that way when only 100% was required. So, you see sometimes it is not all about training. Sometimes it is about having common sense, and about your attitude.

If you wear a Badge. Have you ever thought to ask yourself: Am I that person with the Badge or am I a Beast? Am I the one who started out with good intentions to uphold the Law to Serve and Protect or am I the Beast? Am I the one who started out with good intentions, but due to job stress, dealing with other people's problems, seeing death up close, investigating homicides, suffering from burn-out,' etc. have now become that Beast? Am I the one who will gun down a human being, when my life is not in danger or the one who will beat someone into submission without justification feeling no emotion? Is it me who will take out frustrations and problems on another human being, via, physical or mental tactics and feel justified because I wear the uniform and have perception on my side? Am I the Beast?

Has the Officer become insensitive to his/her family and spouses' feelings, needs and drifted away from basic moral attributes and standards of humanity such as simply treating people like he/she wants to be treated? Yes, I again ask, Badge or Beast.

I would, at this time, like to tell you about a true story involving a not so good COP. Before I go into the details, I want to again remind you that sometimes, wearing a Badge can be a prestigious thing. It's true, whether people like to admit it or not. COPs sometimes get easier loans from banks, get half priced meals. Get traffic tickets voided. Get more traffic warnings than tickets. Yes, Badge or Beast.

Getting back to the not so good COP issue. There is nothing worse than a bad COP. A Bad COP is certainly, in my eyes, a Beast. I worked as a Police Officer in a small community whose population were primarily all black. I worked with a very bad COP. This individual was incredible. Like I say, there's nothing worse than a bad COP (Beast with a Badge.) This bad COP would rob, steal and stop drug dealers. Take their guns, drugs and money and keep it for himself and his own use.

One night he stopped a car and confiscated guns (.25 and .45 caliber semi-automatic weapons) from some young men. Instead of turning the guns in, as found/confiscated property. He gave the Pearl Handle .25 caliber gun to a rookie and he kept the .45 caliber gun for himself. The next day he came to the department bragging about the pistol, which he had bought new grips for, and showed it to me, and asked, "How do you like it?" I asked, "Where did you get that gun?" He replied, with a smile, "Don't worry about it, it's mine God Damn-it!"

About a week later, the Sheriff's Department, Homicide Investigators came to the department and spoke with the Chief, reference to one of his Officers confiscating a Murder Weapon. Needless to say, the Chief didn't know what they were talking about. The Chief gathered us together (all three of us) and stated rather firmly and angrily. "Someone from this agency did a 10-50 (vehicle stop) and confiscated some property." "You have four hours to get it turned-in." Not until that speech did I know what was going on with the .45 caliber pistol. What happened was a man was murdered at a Mall (shot in the forehead) while walking out of the Woolworth Department Store. The murder victim was a known drug dealer and it is believed that his murder was the result of a hit (planned murder.)

The Sheriff's Department had arrested a suspect for the murder. He later confessed and told the investigators a Police Officer had stopped him and confiscated money, drugs and two handguns. The Officer he mentioned was very well educated, had a Criminal Justice Degree. However, somewhere in his life, he developed a drug habit. I believe this had a lot to do in converting him from Badge to Beast.

Instead of the bad COP turning in the confiscated property. He gave the Pear Handle .25 caliber to the rookie and kept everything else for himself. Like I said, the bad COP was very intelligent to get out of this situation. He placed the blame on the Rookie Officer.

This is what happened. The Rookie Officer approached me and told me about stopping the car with the bad COP. He told me that he was aware of the .45 caliber pistol and he stated he was scared he would get fired if the Chief knew about it. I advised him to turn- in the pistol he was given. And write it up as found property. I also advised him to try and convince the bad COP to do the same.

After he spoke with the bad COP. The bad COP convinced the rookie to turn in both weapons and tell the chief that he made a mistake and was intended to turn-in the weapons. However, due to the stress and pressures of training, he forgot about them.

The Chief was satisfied with the report and he was happy the murder weapon was recovered. He also was satisfied that he could strike the incident off as a rookie mistake and still save face with the Sheriff's Department.

Unfortunately, there were other incidents involving the bad COP. I don't mean to dwell on this issue much longer. However, I do feel that it's important for people to know that there are a few bad COPs out there who has gone from Badge to Beast.

Another incident that I recall is where I responded to a house fire to assist with crowd control. Upon my arrival, the fire department was already on the scene, and so was the bad COP. I was called away from the fire scene to investigate an automobile accident involving the lady whose house had been burned. Her daughter was driving at a high rate of speed in order to get to school to inform her sister that their house was on fire. However, she wrecked her mom's car. The daughter was okay, but the car was totaled. The woman's house was on fire and her car was wrecked all in a matter of approximately thirty minutes.

After the fire was extinguished and the vehicle accident investigation was complete, I returned to the department and the bad COP (who was Acting Chief at the time) was in the office with the door locked. I asked, "what are you doing locked up in there?" He started laughing and replied, "don't worry about it." Shortly afterwards, his shift ended, and he went home. I received a call to return to the scene of the fire. This was approximately 9:00 pm. I met a middle-aged lady who was very distraught. She looked as if she was about to have a nervous breakdown. Her house had been burned and the car was wrecked.

I looked at her and she very nervously stated, "When my house was on fire. I told the officer (bad COP), I had some money on my night table and I wanted him to get it for me." "I had $700.00 cash in one envelope and $2,200.00 cash in another." "I was saving some of the money for my son, who is in the military service." "The other money, I was saving to add a room to my home." She went on to state, "the officer gave me the envelope with the $700.00 but not the envelope with the $2,200.00." He had told her that the money burned up in the fire. She stated, "Sir, I know he has to have it because they were right there together. If one was burnt up, then the other one would have burned." "Sir, please get it for me, I need my money and I know he has it."

I felt, at the time, very sorry for this woman. I rushed back to the station and went in to talk to the officer, but he had gone. I realized then why he had the door locked earlier because he was counting the money.

I went back to the woman's home and advised her to talk to the Mayor and see if he would launch an investigation towards her allegations. I also advised her there is a possibility the officer could have the money. However, she needed to act as soon as possible. The officer, in question, was also the Acting Chief of Police. So, she couldn't go to him and ask for her money back. The next day the bad COP came into the Police Department with new clothes, a cigar in his mouth. New equipment and so on. I asked, "where did you get the money to buy all of that stuff?" He jokingly replied, "Don't worry about it." I told him that the woman said she is missing $2,200.00. I asked him, "Man! Did you take her money?" He, again, smiled and said, "man you're crazy."

A couple of days later. The dispatcher (who happened to be the bad COP's friend) told me he had made a deposit at the bank. I told the dispatcher what had happened, and he wasn't at all surprised. He knew how bad the COP was. I continued to work with the woman on trying to get her money back. I believe she ended up getting it back from her insurance policy.

Getting back to the book Badge or Beast. I still say there is nothing worst or should I say no Beast with a Badge worse than a bad COP. I would like to remind you that all the scenarios in this book are true. Badge or Beast. What makes a person, or should I say a person with a Badge go bad?

Let's continue a little with the bad COP. This particular COP eventually got hired with another Police Department. It is alleged that he took his thieving ways with him. His new location became suspicious and allegedly he was set up by the Department.

They placed a wallet in a phone booth and dispatched the call for him to recover the wallet. He responded and recovered the money. When he returned to the station, the money was missing from the wallet. It is believed that he stole it. However, the mistake was that no one actually saw him take it. It is unknown if the money was marked or not.

This particular COP ended up robbing a convenience store. It was alleged he walked into the convenience store, picked up the entire cash register and left the store with it. The cash register was later found in a ditch. The finger prints which were taken from the cash register matched the bad COP and he was also identified by the clerk. He was arrested but was not given prison time. He was given probation with the stipulation of entering a drug rehabilitation center and he had to perform community service. I will mention a few more scenarios involving bad COPs because it is important in helping you understand that some COPs are just bad people, and some are changed by the job. There are many issues pertaining to going from Badge to Beast.

I once observed a Police Officer beat a guy unmercifully. It wasn't a racial thing. The officer was black and so was the citizen. I say citizen because the guy was not under arrest. He hadn't even committed a crime.

I was working with an officer at the Police Department when a young black guy came in and asked for his property to be returned to him. The property was a designer stick with African Art carved all over the stick. It was shaped like a walking cane.

The officer had previously confiscated the stick because, for one, he didn't like the guy, and for two, he was in a position to take it from him. His excuse, or should I say, his justification was the stick could have been used as a weapon. The officer continued to delay giving the citizen his property, just for the hell-of-it. The citizen asked the officer for the stick, rather nicely. However, the officer refused. As the citizen was exiting the Police Station, he mumbled, rather angrily, "Fat A_ _, Mother f_ _ _ _ _!" The COP became so enraged, he grasped the-citizen by the collar of his shirt and literally beat him to a pulp. The officer lost it. He was like a "pit bull." The only way I could stop him from beating the citizen was to "Mace" him and the citizen, both. I couldn't, or should I say wouldn't directly "Mace" the officer in the eyes (as a common courtesy) although I should have.

After I had maced them both. The officer released the citizen in order to rinse his eyes out. When the officer released the citizen, I gave the citizen some water to rinse his eyes with. He stated he wanted to file a complaint. I advised him to return in the morning to speak with the Chief, in reference to filing a Citizens' Complaint. I later spoke with the officer and asked him, why he had lost his temper the way he did. The officer replied, "I always loose it when someone calls me "FAT"." "It's a complex I've always had." In reality, the officer really was "Fat" (300 plus pounds.)

That's what I call my classic eyewitness example to Police Brutality. The list of bad COPs goes on and on. There was the COP who set his car on fire to cover a crime scene. Then there was this bizarre Trooper in a county in Florida who, I'm told by a confidential source, picked up "Hitch Hikers." The Trooper would take their bodies to a remote wooded area, kill them and return a few days later to have intercourse with the decomposed bodies. He had what we would call "Necrophilia."

I would like to address the issue of why, I think the divorce rate of officers and those who work in the field of Law Enforcement/Corrections is so high. The reason is because on a daily basis, they must not only deal with their own problems, but the problems of others. They see things every day, without filters, that the average person only sees maybe once or twice in a life time. For example, an accident with someone decapitated. An accident where small children have been killed. Investigating a scene where a decomposed body has been for days or months. These types of things causes a different kind of stress. Officers must make jokes about the accidents that are so severe that it may cause an officer to lose his/her mind (sanity) it they didn't have an outlet or make humor out of a tragic situation.

I would like to mention some real-life incidents which have affected me and my situation at home. While working with another Department, I received a call relating to a Signal-7 (Dead Person). This "dead person" was a child. I arrived at the home and a young black woman who was very distraught, met me. I asked her what had happened, and she escorted me to the back bedroom. She pointed towards the front of the bed.

I saw one of the most beautiful infant's I had ever seen. He had dark curly hair. He was only two months old. I looked at him lying on the pillow. I suspected that he was dead because the paramedics had arrived before me and the call came over the radio as a Signal-7. When I looked at the baby, it had blood coming from the nostrils. I didn't have any children at the time, so I couldn't fully relate to the grief the woman was going through at the time. I asked her what had happened, and she replied, "I laid him down next to me, on his back, on the pillow at approximately 10:00pm last night. When I awoke at approximately 5:00 A.M., I noticed he wasn't breathing. I also noticed he was on his stomach with blood coming from his nostrils.

In my own mind, I thought the child possibly suffocated during the night when his head turned, face down, into the pillow while his mother slept lying next to him. It appeared as though he was not strong enough to lift his head from the pillow. However, I kept my thoughts to myself pending an investigation and examination by the Medical Examiner, who was on the scene. The Medical Examiner ruled the death as "SIDS" (Sudden Infant Death syndrome.)

As a Law Enforcement Officer, Corrections Officer, you are trained to suppress your feelings and emotions. As for the concern of the child, it really bothered me, he had died exactly on his second month birthday. What bothered me even more, was this poor child never had a chance to experience the fullness of life. I couldn't get this incident out of my head. I went home, and I didn't want to talk to my wife about it because for one, I didn't like talking about my work at home and for the second reason, she and I had been trying to have a child and we were having difficulties. I didn't want to upset her with something as tragic as that. Even today, years later, I think about that poor little child and the fact that he didn't get a chance to grow-up.

After our son was born, I made sure he slept in his own crib, lying on his stomach. Every time he made the smallest noise, during the night, I was right there. This was due to the fear of him dying, during the night, of S.I.D.S. My point is this, the stress which I suffer from is related to this one call. This has caused me many years of job stress. Even long after my employment with the Police Department had ended.

Another incident which bothered me emotionally and caused me great stress. I was working for a Police Department and was driving behind a vehicle. When I observed the driver swerving across the road. I pulled the car over to the right shoulder of the road and stopped. I saw a person jerking and thrashing about in the driver's seat of the car. I thought the person was having a seizure.

I called dispatch to send out Fire and Rescue, who responded within minutes. They started C.P.R. on the person and tried to resuscitate but with negative results. What I thought was a seizure, I later found out, was a massive heart attack. I was not supposed to, but I notified the next of kin. That was stressful in itself. I first called his job and his co-workers, but they could not give me any information about him because he was going through a divorce. I finally contacted his father who was living in Orange County California. It was a sad moment, telling his father that his son had passed away. I started thinking, "Man! That could have been me." It took about two weeks for me to fully get it out of my mind.

What I'm discussing now are true incidents which I encountered that caused me great stress. Also, some of these incidents caused me to become hardened and insensitive to certain issues. There also was no one whom I felt I could talk through these feelings. Sometimes my wife would notice a change and ask, "what's wrong?" I would sometimes snap by responding, "Nothing! I just don't want to be bothered." In reality, I most likely saw a dead person that day or weekend.

Sometimes I would be called an insensitive S.O.B. I don't care what an officer says, the job changes you. It doesn't matter how long he has been working the streets. There is always that one incident which will make you break down. It will make you, yes even that big, strong, bad guy, with the badge, break down and cry. If not, you are a great candidate for Badge or Beast. If you think it won't affect you, you are wrong.

Holding in stress will cause you several problems. I recall the incident in town. When a Haitian Male decapitated a five-year-old boy head off with an axe. All because the child's Mother was sending him to live with his real father in New

York. The Deputy who responded saw the blood and the child's head chopped off and he broke down and started crying. He could not handle this situation without feeling remorse for the child. I don't know, maybe he had kids at home. I, again, want to emphasize the fact that those tough officers/people with a Badge. If they don't break down sometime, or just hold it in, they stand a good chance of transforming from Badge to Beast. Are you one of those candidates? Have you noticed a change in your personality from soft to hard? Or should I say from Badge to Beast.

This brings to mind the incident to which I responded, involving the death of a beautiful young female. She was approximately 28 years of age. She allegedly died from having a Grand Mal Seizure. When I arrived, her parents greeted me at the door. They were elderly. Both were very distraught, especially the Mother. I asked what had happened. And her Father stated, "She had seizures." "She had a seizure and went into convulsions." "She never recovered." She died as a result of the convulsions.

I looked at her lying on the sofa. She appeared as though she was a sleep. I said, to myself, "God! She's so pretty." "She looks too beautiful to die." I felt that way for two reasons. The first reason was I had great sympathy for her elderly parents. I was thinking, "Dear God, how are these people going to deal with all of this grief"?" The second reason was that I wanted to grieve, because she was approximately my age. I thought, "Man! She is so young, that could have been me." However, I'm the guy with the Badge. NO WAY, NOT THIS BIG OFFICER! As bad as I wanted to sit there and cry with the family. I couldn't, my job was to get information and write a report, not grieve with the family.

This added years of stress to my life. I did cry, yeah, but not at the scene. I cried when I left. My image was not shattered. My emotions went tumbling down when I left the scene. This is what I am talking about, when I say, situations can really change and affect the personality of Law Enforcement Officers. Holding stress in, keeping that cool, calm image under pressure. Helps give you heart attacks, diabetes, high blood pressure.

Let me share another story with you in regard to a situation which would make the average person a mental case. A female Deputy was patrolling a remote area of the county. She drove up on a parked vehicle. She got out of her patrol car to investigate the vehicle. She looked inside but could not see, due to the windows being all fogged and dirty. She called for back-up, due to the remote area and the suspicious nature of the incident. When back-up arrived, they managed to open the door of the car and what they saw was gruesome. A man had shot his brains out with a shotgun. The reason she could not see inside initially, was because the man's brains were scattered all over the inside of his vehicle. Needless to say, the deputy decided to enter a different line of work after this incident. I have come home from work, so stressed out, I didn't want to talk to anyone, not even my wife.

The next story is about stress so severe that the Officer almost snapped. He responded to a call (house fire) to assist. It was believed the fire was a result of Arson. A young, Chemical Engineer, was distraught over breaking up with his teenage girl friend. Obviously unstable, he allegedly made the comment, "If I can't have you, nobody else will." One night, he allegedly threw a fire bomb through the young girl's bedroom window and she and her thirteen-year-old sister were killed. I believe she was only nineteen years old. It was such a senseless tragedy. It was also tragic to witness a double funeral of these young and beautiful sisters.

When I spoke with the Officer, he told me that when he arrived, he saw the girls standing at the bedroom window screaming. He reached in, to try and grab them, but the fire was too hot. He said he tried several times, to no avail. The Officer told me that following the incident, he ended up in a beach area in Florida without knowing how or when he got there. He stated that his wife didn't even know where he was. His mind went totally blank. I believe if he had not gotten away, he would have gone absolutely crazy. Stress kills and has destroyed many marriages. Officers fall victim to divorce and sometimes suicide when only one partner in the relationship is a member of Law Enforcement. It is difficult, if not impossible to communicate verbally, the depth of stress encountered and anyone who is not engaged in this line of work really can't fully understand.

I know up to this point, I have primarily discussed incidents involving Police Officers and people with Badges who work primarily in the city, county and state. I would now like to share with you incidents involving the Corrections Field. There are many, many types of correctional institutions federal, state and county. In Law Enforcement/Corrections, the stress of wearing a Badge, no matter the level or location, can be just as devastating as that of a Police Officer on the street.

Employability as a Corrections Officer has State requirements of numerous years of training. Then there's the background checks, and in some, if not all cases, you have to perform a psychological evaluation. This all takes place before you are hired if you are one of the lucky ones. Once hired, there is the added stress of being placed on probation before you are accepted as a full-time employee. However, let us get to the meat of the matter. It takes a special kind (breed) of person to work in a Correctional environment, on a county level.

What I would like to discuss is some of the things that a Corrections Officer goes through. I'm not going to elaborate much on the administrative end. Although, I will from time to time discuss issues which can and does add to job stress. What I'm going to talk about, primarily, is from a Correctional Officer's point of view or should I say, real "jail world" issues. These are the day to day issues, dealing with, and working directly with inmates.

I started my career in Corrections in May of 1983. I had experience as a COP, so I thought Corrections would be pretty much the same. Boy, was I wrong. Once I finished the months of pretesting and the long process of evaluations, etc. I found out that Corrections is just as stressful as Law Enforcement. I first want to talk about job related stresses within the jail environment. Then I'm going to talk about real life experiences and actual live cases of incidents involving Corrections and the jail environment. All of the things I'm about to relate to are not all going to be negative. However, just like a news reporter, and a newspaper, people want to hear and read about the good and the bad stuff, you know, the blood and guts kind of thing. So, let us get to the meat of the matter.

While working in a Correctional Facility, within a County system, I have learned a lot about life and the jail environment. To introduce you to the real world of the jail. I would first like to say that 50% to 60% of the people who get hired to work in the jail, after one to six months, show a drastic change in personality. As for myself, well I can also say it is true. However, it took me approximately one and a half years. I can honestly say that this job has cause me to be less sensitive to people emotions. No, I didn't say I was a cold blooded, nasty person. I said I wasn't as sensitive (emotionally) as I used to be. Now, to get to the heart of the issue.

A Corrections Officer or anyone who deals directly with inmates in a jail environment can relate to what I'm about to tell you in this book. Some of these incidents may be hard to accept if you are not accustomed to working in the jail. I must say that all of the incidents I'm about to address, are true experiences. I will change the names to protect the innocent.

I speak to you with over twenty-five years of experience. Let us get on with the book. I would like for you, at this time, if you work for Law Enforcement/Corrections, etc. Ask yourself, honestly, are you an Officer with a Badge? Or are you a Beast?

Like many of my counter-parts who started a career in Law Enforcement, I wanted a position to help people. It was also secure with a certain amount of power and prestige that goes along with the job. Many people start in Corrections using it as a "stepping stone" to work their way up to be a COP. I did just the opposite. I started as a COP with a City agency and now presently work as a Corrections Officer with a County agency. The point I'm trying to make, is that I've worked both sides of the system (Law Enforcement and Corrections), so I know what I'm talking about.

When I first started in Corrections, I had to make the transition from the streets to inside of the jail. In the process, I had to first get use to the politics which goes on inside of the Correctional Institution. It can be stressful watching people get promoted because someone liked them, not because they're the best qualified for the job. I know, that happens in most work places. But, let's get back to the story. In talking about actual job-related stress.

The average citizen has no idea what goes on behind the bars and doors of a jail. There is homosexuality, which is sometimes seen as normal. There are fights between inmates over other inmates, etc. Correctional staff, both male and female sometimes fall in love with inmates. Some have gone so far as to get married to the inmate. The inmates that I work with are very cunning. They really try to con women officers into falling in love with them; some actually succeed. I relay some of these facts so that you understand the backdrop under which Correctional Officers work on a day to day basis. These actions contribute to the stress factor. Again, I want you to know that I'm speaking from experience.

This book should help people understand what goes on inside of a Correctional Institution. It should help spouses, friends and loved ones of Correctional Officers to understand some of the things they must go through. Knowing the environment in which Correctional Officers work will help the inner circle of family and friends deal with the stress, the mood swings, the insensitivity and sometimes, downright rude attitude of Correctional Officers. This environment is not like the TV glamor of jail or prison, but the reality of what Corrections work is really like.

Many of my co-workers are divorced. I think this is due to the stress of the job. I remember an Officer who worked in a particular area of the jail (Psychological Unit). He was having problems with his girlfriend on the outside. One day he completely lost it. He walked off the job, dropped his keys off at the control room and left the facility. He continued to walk down a major highway and headed for Daytona. I don't know, but rumor has it he was partially clothed. The stress was too much, he just lost it. This may seem extreme and some of you may say that there should be regular psych exams for members of Law Enforcement. There are, however these Psychological exams only work when the Officer is completely honest about what he or she is feeling and open to deal with the issues at hand.

I remember the time when I experienced my first inmate death. This caused much stress on me, because I continued to think about it, even after I got off work and went home. The inmate was a young male, approximately twenty-two years old. He was alleged to have been a former drug user. He had a massive, fatal heart attack while lying in his bunk.

My supervisor called me to give C.P.R. However, another Officer had already started C.P.R. by the time I arrived. The inmate continued to turn darker and darker. I knew he was dying, because of his skin color. He was getting no oxygen. Needless to say, he died at the hospital. There is an old saying, within the jail system, "No one ever dies in the jail." This is said, due to the liability factor. If someone actually dies in the jail, the full liability and responsibility of the inmate's death lies with the institution and agency.

I thought about this young kid and how tragic it was to die at such an early age. I also thought about his parents and family and I had such sympathy for them. Although he was an inmate, incarcerated within the jail system, he was still a human being, who had family which cared for him and loved him. This type of stress causes an Officer to not want to talk to his own family members when they get near. Who wants to talk, when you have experienced death first hand? Keeping these feeling pinned up inside, actually causes more stress than talking about it. This leads me to discuss another incident which caused me great stress. It was not an inmate death, but an escape. This is something about which every Officer has nightmares.

In February of 1985, an inmate escaped from the "Trustee" area of the jail. The inmate had only a few months before he was to be released or so the jail thought. In reality, he was facing about ten years in another state and Classification failed to find it out. Remember that in 1985, the level of technology that we have today did not exist. So, based on incomplete/inaccurate information, this Trustee-Inmate was housed in a minimum-security housing area. He was given permission to work a double shift by a Lieutenant (which was against policy). He escaped between 9:00 pm and Midnight.

I was working the Modular Control Room at the time of the escape. Because I was on duty at the time of the incident, I ended up getting a two-day suspension along with three other Officers and Supervisors. The Lieutenant, who was responsible for allowing the inmate to work the two shifts, did not receive any discipline, (politics within the system). Needless to say, this caused me much stress. I felt the Lieutenant should have been the only one who received any discipline because it was his unauthorized decision that allowed the inmate to work a double shift. The Correctional Officers who were punished actually had nothing to do with the decisions that led to the escape.

The day I received my discipline. My wife and I were on our way down south, for a vacation. At the time, she was pregnant with my son. She had been experiencing morning sickness, but we were determined to get away for a few days for some well-deserved rest and recuperation. I was just about to leave and get on the Turnpike to head south. It was about 8:00 am, on Friday, when I received my call to go to the Captain's Office for my discipline. I was furious when they told me I was being suspended for two days for my involvement in the escape. I made it clear to administration that I felt I was being used as a "scapegoat." If the Lieutenant hadn't given permission for the inmate to work the double shift, I would not have given permission for the Trustee to be away from the housing area. I accepted the discipline and continued on my vacation, mad as h_ _ _ and all stressed out because I felt I was being punished for someone else's mistake. Great vacation.

Now can you understand the stress of being investigated and punished, especially for an inmate's escape. I must stay focused on the Book "Badge or Beast". I remember when an inmate (Psychological Inmate) plucked both his eyes out. The responding Officer looked for but could not find one of the eyes. The other eye was hanging out and the inmate was pulling on the eyeball and the cord it was connected to. He was trying to pull it out. The Officer said he could see the inmate's brain. We believe the inmate stepped on the other eye as we never did find it. The doctors ended up sewing both his eyelids shut. Needless to say, the inmate is permanently blind.

The inmate in this incident was incarcerated for raping an elderly lady. He had cut off both her arms and legs after he raped and strangled her to death. On the morning he plucked both of his eyes out, Officers say he was reading the Bible. It is believed he was reading the scriptures, "An eye for an eye, a tooth for a tooth." "If you offend your neighbor, pluck your eyes out." Well, you have to find a little humor, in the midst of tragedy, otherwise, you may go insane thinking about it.

In dealing with stressful situations. People handle it differently, in their own way. I can't help it, when I experience a tragic situation, it takes a minimum of two days to get it out of my system. It takes even longer to get it out of my memory. There are situations which I've encountered during my Law Enforcement/Corrections career which I will never forget. For instance, the inmate who had AIDS. He complained all day about his body hurting all over. He was taken to the hospital the previous day for testing. They knew he had liver damage.

After the test, he was returned to the facility. During the evening shift, he started complaining again about his body hurting all over. The nurse came by and evaluated him. She checked his vital signs and everything appeared alright. However, around 7:30 pm that same evening, his cell mate came to the door and stated, "My roommate isn't breathing, I think he's dead." When I arrived, all the other inmates were locked down. The Officer had started C.P.R. He was giving breaths with the ambu-bag. To make a long story short, the inmate died and was turning blue, right before my very eyes.

The Paramedics arrived and the moment we told them the inmate had AIDS, they did not touch him. They left him lying right on the floor (on display) for everyone to see. Normally, Paramedics would remove the body and transport it to the hospital. However, they wanted nothing to do with the body. The inmates body stayed on the floor, in the cell, until the Medical Examiner arrived and officially declared the inmate dead. I still think about it, sometimes, it really bothers me thinking about the body, lying on the floor, blue, with green and black bile dripping out of his mouth and running down the side of his face, on the floor. That is stress.

The average person could not deal with a situation like that. Some of the staff had to have psychological counseling because they were on the scene and watched the inmate literally die right in front of them. Also, some of the staff had to get medical testing done because not only did the inmate have AIDS, he also had hepatitis. Fortunately, none of the staff tested positive. Speaking of medical issues within the Corrections environment, there are times when medical knows of an inmate's condition and will not advise the staff of the medical condition of the inmate.

Yeah, I know, medical histories are confidential. (HIPPA) However, wouldn't you want to know if a person has Tuberculosis, if you come in contact with that person on a regular basis, especially if you have small children? There are instances when we have worked with inmates for weeks and all of a sudden, medical advises us we have to quarantine an inmate because they suspect he/she may have a contagious disease. What kind of rights do we, as Corrections Officers, have? Obviously, none.

Imagine the stress of coming into contact with these people when you have small children at home, especially if you have a new born infant. The stress that comes with working in a Correctional environment is high because the system seems to be geared towards the inmate and those who put their lives on the line daily. It seems as though administration cares more about inmates than their own staff. Even though we get to go home after our shift, we too sometimes feel that we are prisoners at a different level.

If you work in a Law Enforcement/ Corrections environment, have you noticed that you may experience a personality change? Have you sensed that you are somewhat falling away from your spirituality? If you are a Christian, do you sometimes feel that this job is not the job for you? Well, if you don't feel that way, I do. Due to working in the jail, I have noticed a definite weakening in my spirituality. There's something about the environment. I can't fully explain it, but I would like to try.

If you're involved in Law Enforcement/ Corrections, you probably will understand what I'm about to say. When I first started in Corrections, I was very much into my religion. I don't speak much about it because my faith is very personal to me. However, I feel that now is the time to talk about this. I've never even discussed it with my wife. I didn't think she would understand. She is going to know now because she will read it in the Book. I started Corrections as a meek, humble, very spiritual man.

Approximately one year later I noticed a drastic change in my spirituality. No, I'm not that Beast that I mention in this Book. I'm just sharing very personal experiences with you. I was raised and brought up in a very spir1tual environment. I attended church. My church has a very strict Doctrine. There once was a time when women in my church were not allowed to wear pants or make-up. Children were not allowed to go to the movies or play school sports. You get the picture.

After about a year and a half, I was assigned to work in another part of the jail that was a much harsher environment. I encountered an inmate who was very belligerent and just plain ignorant. He wanted to go to the Law Library. Administration had issued an order (Policy) that only twenty inmates would be allowed to go to the library. The limit was reached. The inmate asked if he could go. I advised him that there was a twenty-person limit and the limit was reached. He became irate and belligerent and stated, "I want a grievance for my being refused the Law Library." "You are violating my Civil Rights." I advised him again, that the Law Library was full and he would have to wait until tomorrow. He insisted he get a grievance form. I gave him one.

You have to understand; some inmates think that filing a grievance form against staff will get staff fired. I really got upset when the inmate started cursing me out, using profanity, stating, "All you F _ _ _ _ _ _ Officers are alike, you all don't give a F_ _ _ about inmates." "That's why I'm going to fill out this grievance form on you and get your nigger A_ _ fired."

Here I was being honest with him; advising him of the new policy and he didn't believe me. He wanted what he wanted and didn't care to believe me. I find that attitude and mentality with inmates who have a history of drug use (Junkies.) I became angry and disappointed with this particular inmate because I was really sincere and honest in telling him the truth, yet his main objective was to get me fired. I abruptly and angrily told him that I didn't care if he filed a grievance and furthermore there was no way he could get me fired.

At that time, I felt very angry and I experienced something that to this day don't understand. I felt a weakening in my spirituality and I really felt like grabbing that particular inmate around the mid-section and slamming him. That is not my nature. I knew it was against Policy and Procedures. So, I just looked at him, gritted my teeth and suppressed my anger, hostility and revengeful emotions. In that moment I felt like the Beast. I think at some point in every Officer's career, if they work in detention, they will experience this same feeling. There's going to be that one inmate who drives you to the point (even if it's briefly) to where you honestly want to do bodily harm. Some Officers are unable to suppress the evil emotions. Those are the ones who eventually get investigated for excessive use of force.

Being a Christian, I constantly train myself and internally battle the emotions of hurting someone. In other words, many Officers, based on irate inmates, job and family stress, allow themselves to become the Beast. They become that person who can no longer control their anger, the one who gets pleasure in giving inmates pain. The inmates who violate policy, who deliberately push staff to the breaking point, are the ones that some staff look forward to breaking down. Yes, they push Officers until eventually, the Beast will surface, and you have to control it and recognize your stress breaking point.

Back to the lecture at hand... Yes, I personally experienced the Beast and Stress Breaking Point. However, since that day, I lost a lot of respect for inmates. What I mean by that is their behavior and level of disrespect to Officers made me think twice about going out of my way to do things for them. I would do only those things which are minimally required by law (Florida Administrative Code 33-8.) To this day, I remember that incident very vividly because it interfered with my family life. It brought on a personality change in me that I did not like, nor did my wife. It was totally out of character for me.

When I first married in 1978, I was a very spiritual man, all of my emotions (intimate and otherwise) were centered around my wife. Since the experience with the irate inmate, my wife noticed a change in my spirituality. She often asked, "Are you still a Christian and why don't you go to church like you use to?" "Are you still saved?" I always avoided the answer, just like I avoided the conversation with her in regard to this incident and the spiritual weakening. Instead, I lashed out at her. I asked her, "Are you saved and why are you worried about me?" "Live your spiritual life for you because a relationship with Christ is a personal one, so worry about yourself." I was only avoiding the issue relating to my spirituality. I never discussed this issue with her because I felt that she wouldn't understand. I felt that she would only criticize me. Using phrases, such as, "You're only a hypocrite." "You "Holy Rollers" are always being a phony." You see, I come from a Pentecostal background (stricter.)

She watched me very closely in my everyday walk with Christ. So, she knew when I experienced a spiritual weakening. She noticed me not studying my Bible as intensely as I used to. She noticed me not attending church services as I had previously. She noticed a change in my music (singing, song writing and performing.) She noticed me writing about more worldly things instead of spiritual things.

You see, I carried/carry the stress of not talking about that experience, not dealing with reality. In writing this book, I feel like I've lifted a burden from my shoulders that I've carried around for years because in not talking about this issue, I let it fester in my spirit. There is healing in writing this book, not just for others but for myself as well. Stress and the suppression of these feelings are some of the reasons for so many divorces in the Law Enforcement/Corrections field. I hope by sharing my experiences someone will recognize the importance of sharing information with your spouse or your loved ones.

Many times, the people in our lives, our partners in marriages, members of our families, personal and professional relationships, the people we date, don't know what the issues are that we are dealing with and feel that they may be at fault. Open communication is critical to the health of any relationship but especially your marriage. The reality is that it's not them. It's all the "other stuff" that gets in the way of having good, solid relationships.

Okay, enough about myself. The book, Badge or Beast, means a lot to me. Ironically, remember the incident in front of the book, where the white Officer shot a black suspect in the back with a shotgun (for nothing.) I recently found out that he made Sergeant. Now that, to me, was a real slap in the face and to all minority citizens of the city where he works. Not only did he get promoted. He's teaching a (Liability) class at a Criminal Justice Institute.

I guess he would know about liability. He shot and killed an innocent person. He got time off, with pay. He was then promoted to Sergeant. It's really sad. Well, I guess I might as well get this joke in: "What do you call a Black Man in a brand-new house?" "A Burglar." You see, that's the mentality of many, so called professional officers who are supposed to uphold the law for all citizens. That racist joke was told to me by a Spanish officer who considers himself white. No wonder there are so many Beasts on the streets and in the institutions, with Badges.

Think about it. Are you a professional with a Badge? Or are you a Beast? Waiting for the opportunity to explode emotionally. Waiting for the opportunity to take another human life? To beat the living daylights out of another human being. All because you were placed in a position of trust to uphold the law. At some stage in your career, you changed, and you discovered that you are afraid to accept the change, to deal with it by getting counseling (if needed... it's free.) Oh! No! The Big Bad Criminal Justice Person, the unemotional, uncaring of other people's needs member of Law Enforcement cannot seek help and maintain the perception of strength... or at least that is what we think. That is what keeps us bottled up on the inside, our fear of how we will be perceived by those outside of Law Enforcement/Corrections as well as our co-workers.

That one Officer, who's looking for an excuse to step outside of "Serve and Protect" finds it in all the stressful situations that we are surrounded by. I can go on and on and on about the negative incidents involving Criminal Justice personnel. I choose not to do so at this time. I would like to write a movie script from this Book one day and show the perspective of a member of Law Enforcement who is willing to tell the truth about the emotional effects of this work. I believe it is important to show the world how dangerous it is to work within the Criminal Justice System, not just physically but emotionally. This is one line of work that can literally, I mean literally, change an innocent, up standing, law abiding citizen, into one of the most dangerous persons in the world.

In conclusion, I challenge you, Mr. Police Officer, Mr. Corrections Officer, Mr. Criminal Justice Person, whoever you are. To up hold the law and preserve mankind in a manner which allows you to proudly say, "I am a person with a *BADGE* and not the person who is the *BEAST*."

THE BEGINNING

NOT THE END

www.ingramcontent.com/pod-product-compliance
Lightning Source LLC
Chambersburg PA
CBHW070035040426
42333CB00040B/1681